# Encountering

# Charismatic

# Worship

by

## Colin Buchanan

*Vice-Principal of St. John's College, Bramcote, Nottingham*
*Member of the Church of England Liturgical Commission*

## GROVE BOOKS

## BRAMCOTE NOTTS.

# CONTENTS

## FOREWORD

I have been encouraged to put this book together by the response of the Group for Renewal of Worship to an outline I presented to it. But my major debt is to the many persons with whom I have worshipped over the years, and particularly to the staff and students of St. John's College. I would like to thank three current students—Dave Bowler, Dave Butterfield and Colin McCormack—for their especial help. The resultant booklet is a typically hasty product, and it bears the marks of May 1977 strongly upon it. It may well date quickly in a fast-moving stiuation. And certainly it cannot pretend to be more than one man's view of moving events.

C.O.B. 20 May 1977

*First Impression* May 1977

**ISSN** 0305 3067
**ISBN** 0 905422 11 2

# 1. INTRODUCTION

In one sense this booklet is a great joy to write. It comes from living experience at St. John's College, where I both teach 'worship' to the students, and learn worship from them. It comes at a time when for about three years I have been actively involved with Anglican charismatics outside the College in various ways—including conferences, study and participation as a visitor in charismatic parishes. It comes particularly when the April 1977 National Evangelical Anglican Congress is fresh in memory—and 'NEAC' both included, and united, charismatic and non-charismatic evangelicals. It comes when a recent statement uniting these two groups theologically has also been issued.[1] It comes therefore at a time when the signs are that there is no 'charismatic divide' at all, and when lessons may therefore be learned painlessly from each other. It is a happy time at which to write the booklet, and it enables me to express appreciately many things I have been learning in recent years.

On the other hand, I am conscious of two very great difficulties in the project. These are:

1. I am not technically a charismatic (or at least not a 'card-carrying' one!). If I am right that an honest juncture of evangelicals and charismatics has now been reached, then my own history is of little significance *for to-day*. But it *is* relevant to how I have experienced the Charismatic Movement in the past, and I do not pretend that all my own thinking has lost its independence of the Movement (with an occasional polarization from it). I can only claim a modicum of live experience, a certain amount of reading, a good deal of encounter with persons, and a deep desire to interpret what I find. If I have any special qualification to write this booklet it derives from this somewhat journalistic stance[2] rather than from any absolute commitment to the Charismatic Movement as we have known it hitherto. But, on the other hand, it is arguable that somewhere in the discussion ought to come some interpretation from sympathetic observers of the Movement. Otherwise we are dependent upon the starry-eyed success stories of the Movement on the one hand, or uncomprehending ignorance or dismissal of it on the other. If I have any wounds to inflict (and they are few and slight) they are the faithful wounds of a friend.

2. The data are not systematized. I attempt to do a round-up of various distinctive phenomena of charismatic worship, sometimes taking books as my sources, sometimes conversations, sometimes personal

[1] *Gospel and Spirit*, published simultaneously as a *Theological Renewal* occasional paper (and obtainable as a separate publication from the Fountain Trust), and also published as an article in *The Churchman* for April 1977.
[2] Journalism is halfway between propaganda and historiography. It cannot stand back sufficiently to be objective and definitive (and indeed it presupposes that such reporting would be uninteresting!). But there is such a thing as *accurate* journalism, and to that I aspire.

experience. But when that is done the data are relatively few, and are perhaps not as universalizable as my treatment would suggest. Some charismatic parishes exhibit some of the phenomena mentioned here, others exhibit others. But the whole Movement is very new as far as the Church of England is concerned[1], the literature which exists is usually only reporting certain local data (and is strongly inclined towards the stories of individual Christians rather than public worship), and discussion of worship at the level of principle is not as frequent as one might expect. At that, I cannot pretend to have researched exhaustively—this is journalism, not a doctoral thesis— and the reader may well feel I have missed out on something quite central. If so, I am sorry, and would like to know about it. But I am sure it will also be understood that Grove Booklets are intended to stimulate discussion and enquiry, not to terminate it by definitive treatment!

Those reservations expressed, what is the scope of the booklet? I am quite clear about this: it is a survey of the worship of charismatic Anglicans. It is a narrow field. The actual material cannot cover more than a dozen or so years of recent history, nor more than a few dozen actual parishes, nor more than a handful of conferences and other special gatherings. But it would be an impertinence (or a self-evident failure) to try to cover more. And in any case, I soon discovered that I had plenty of material in this narrow compass to fill a Grove Booklet (which, after all, was my aim!), and I content myself with the thought that this, more or less homogeneous, material will itself provide enough questions for both charismatic and non-charismatic readers to tackle immediately. I may also lapse occasionally into exhortation—it is the compulsive habit of the preacher-turned-lecturer who then stops to write.

It is no central part of the project to set out a full history of the Charismatic Movement. Sufficient to note enough points to give a framework for the rest of the booklet:

1. **Pre-history.** The Pentecostal Churches date from the beginning of this century.[2] They have had little impact on the other main denominations, and have tended to be separatist (and sheep-stealing) in relation to the others. The Anglican Churches have had two strands of experience in the earlier part of the twentieth century which have in some way corresponded to pentecostalism, but the differences have been greater than the similarities. These two are, firstly, the 'Keswick' teaching of complete holiness and of a 'second blessing', and secondly, the East Africa Revival movement, which twenty years ago was specifically connected with Ruanda, but is now much more

---

[1] It is with the narrow field of the Charismatic Movement within the Church of England, and particularly as it has affected the evangelical end of the Church of England, that this booklet is concerned. How narrow that is on a world scene can be inferred from Walter Hollenweger's book *The Pentecostals* (SCM, 1972) in which page 186 alone of 572 pages touches on the subject matter of this booklet!

[2] The classic dating is the last night of the Nineteenth Century—see Michael Harper *As At The Beginning* (Hodder, 1965) p.27.

experienced in Kenya, Uganda and Tanzania. It has often been called in England 'Ruanda teaching' and as such it has had direct links with the Keswick strand in England. The theological anticipation of the Charismatic Movement is easy to trace here, but neither Keswick nor the East African Revival have had much effect upon Anglican worship. Even in congregations deeply moved by these influences, the worship would, from the standpoint of 1977, have appeared very traditional. Revival meetings have always been divorced from Anglican Sunday worship (though Revival *sermons* might still be found on Sundays), and this particular background adds little to our recent picture.

2. **Actual History.** The first I ever heard in England was that when I was at Tyndale Hall[1] from 1959 to 1961 it was rumoured that over the Downs at Clifton Theological College there had been, a year or so before, one Dicky Bolt who had had to be asked to leave because he was teaching other students to speak in tongues. I have never checked the story out, it is sufficient that it was very surprising to us that there should have been such a student at an Anglican evangelical theological College, but quite natural (even if sad) that he should have been asked to go![2] Soon after this (in Spring 1962) the *Church of England Newspaper* had headlines 'Tongues at Beckenham'—it was St. Paul's Beckenham, which thus became the first Anglican parish of which I ever heard where these disturbing manifestations took place.[3] Then, in September 1962, I was at the old Oxford Conference of Evangelical Churchmen and heard Philip Hughes, a dyed-in-the-wool Puritan and 'reformed' theologian, speaking with wonder of a new movement of the Spirit (attested by speaking in tongues) amongst—of all people—'high church' American episcopalians.[4] And the matter came much nearer home when a division occurred on the staff of that Mecca-parish of evangelical Anglicans, All Souls Langham Place, and Michael Harper left the staff to found—in 1964—the Fountain Trust. My own first serious encounter with proponents of the Movement was in November 1965 when Dennis Bennett[5] came to the College (then still the London College of Divinity at Northwood) and spoke to the staff and students about what had happened at St. Luke's Seattle where he was rector. I was actually profoundly disappointed with him—he dodged all biblical and theological questions, and said he had simply come to give testimony to what God had done.

1 This was one of the two Anglican Theological Colleges in Bristol which in 1971 combined to become to-day's 'Trinity Theological College'.
2 Pastor Dicky Bolt duly reappears on the stage of history as that which everybody then thought proper he should be—a Pentecostalist minister! See W. Hollenweger *The Pentecostals* (SCM, 1972) p.186.
3 The vicar at the time was one George Forrester, who soon after left the ministry of the Church of England, and started an independent pentecostalist-style assembly near the parish in Bradford where he had previously been the vicar.
4 See W. Hollenweger *op. cit.* p.5; D. Bennett *Nine O'Clock in the Morning* (Coverdale, 1970) *passim;* M. Harper *op. cit.* p.81; P. E. Hughes' editorial in *The Churchman* (September 1962).
5 He of *Nine O'Clock in the Morning* St. Luke's Seattle fame (see footnote 4 above).

After that time the Movement grew slowly, perhaps half-under-ground, through the 1960s[1], and it has flourished, thoroughly above ground, in the 1970s. St. John's College has become a centre to which charismatic ordinands have come for training, and has in more recent years found itself with overtly charismatic staff-members as well as students. To say this is not to say anything exclusive—it is merely to indicate the milieu from which this booklet comes. But this is very much a phenomenon of the 1970s, and it is certainly true in my own life that, although I had occasional encounters with charismatic worship in the 1960s, the great weight of my own experience has been gained in the last three years.

**3. Contextual History.** It would be quite improper to write about charismatic worship as though it were a fast-moving occurrence in an otherwise static church. Anglican readers will hardly need reminding of the general tide of liturgical change which has been running in the last fifteen years, and it is easy to see how this has in most cases given the new insights of the Charismatic Movement a seed-bed in which to grow.

The following features of the tide should be noted:

(i) The Liturgical Movement has grown in the Church of England. In the last fifty years[2] there has sprung up a strong 'Parish Communion' movement and the emphases of this movement are important. There have been: a theory of the church being the body of Christ, with a function for every member; the centrality of holy communion; a gentle world-affirmation; a continuity between life and liturgy; a move towards making ceremonial and setting authentic rather than formal; and a growth of group worship in homes. These features were being discovered by evangelicals (somewhat after many others) in the 1960s[3] and they provided a natural seedbed for charismatic renewal.

[1] I well recall going from 1966 to 1970 to the annual national conferences of the Eclectics Society—a fellowship linking together younger progressive evangelical clergy. Michael Harper was often present, but kept a very low (yes, even semi-underground) profile. The first National Evangelical Anglican Congress at Keele in April 1967 produced a 10000-word statement without any reference to the subject. By then it must have been pretty near the surface!

[2] The 'classic' dating gives a starting-point in December 1927, when St. John's New-castle-upon-Tyne began its '9.15'. See D. M. Paton (ed.) *The Parish Communion To-Day* (S.P.C.K., 1962) p.1; P. Jagger *Henry de Candole: 1897-1971* (Faith Press, 1975) pp.72f; Colin Buchanan *Patterns of Sunday Worship* (Grove Booklet on Ministry and Worship no. 9, 1972 and 1975) p.5.

[3] Despite their traditional love of extempore prayer meetings, evangelicals have always tended to fairly formal (if straightforward) use of both Prayer Book and pulpit in Sunday worship. At Keele in 1967 (see footnote 1 above) they bound themselves to work towards the celebration of communion as the central service of Sunday—but they have not yet moved very far in that direction.

(ii) Textual revision has also come in the last decade.[1] Series 3 Communion in particular, whilst more overtly designed to meet the 'Liturgical Movement' emphases mentioned above, has inevitably also met the desires of many charismatics simply because of their connections (often unacknowledged) with the Liturgical Movement. Series 3 communion offers corporateness, flexibility, joy, informality, and new mention of the body and the Spirit. It has come providentially for charismatics, who have availed themselves of it gladly.

(iii) There was a mood afoot in the Church of England in the early sixties to start experimentation in other ways. Musically, this involved the bringing of guitars (and sometimes of other strings and wind instruments) into worship, even if only on special occasions. New, often ephemeral, Christian songs and hymns started to appear from the Twentieth Century Church Light Music Group, from Sydney Carter, and from many others. Negro spirituals have been revived[2]; new tunes written for old hymns[3]; 'secular' tunes adapted for new lyrics[4]; and whole supplements added to old hymnbooks to collect and conserve the new material.[5] But not only music has been the subject of experimentation. There have also been tried many variants on the traditional sermon as means of communication; and these have included experiments with visual aids, art, drama, dance and even tactual and other experiences. No-one would pretend that these had all been successful, nor that they were necessarily widespread through Anglican parishes. But it would be improper to suggest that the charismatic renewal came into a church completely fossilized in its worship. Rather in general it was to a church engaged on an inarticulate and undirected quest for new life. But in many individual parishes, one must freely acknowledge, the renewal has been wholly new!

[1] The Prayer Book (Alternative and Other Services) Measure 1965 came into force on 1 May 1966, and authorized experimentation and liturgical change dates from then. Series 2 Communion was authorized in July 1967, and Series 3 Communion in November 1972, with effect from 1 February 1973. For details see my *Recent Liturgical Revision in the Church of England* (Grove Booklet on Ministry and Worship no. 14, 1973) and the two *Supplements* to it (no. 14a, 1974, and no. 14b, 1976).

[2] e.g. Joy Webb and the Joystrings (Salvation Army) or the sections on 'Spirituals' at the end of *Youth Praise I* (Falcon, 1966) and *Youth Praise II* (Falcon, 1969), or the ever-popular 'Kum ba yah'.

[3] This is the main (though not exclusive) novelty of the books of the Twentieth Century Church Light Misuc Group (which published largely between 1960 and 1965), and the Michael Brierley tune for 'At the Name of Jesus' and the Geoffrey Beaumont one for 'O Jesus, I have Promised' are typical of those which have passed into general use.

[4] This was General Booth's original idea (I well recall singing a sacred song to 'Drink to me only' the day the Salvation Army led the worship at the Faith and Order Congress here at Nottingham in 1964). It is revived in the use of the Dambusters March (as in *Psalm Praise*, Falcon, 1972), and even (in my limited experience) by the use of the Z Cars theme tune.

[5] As, e.g. *100 Hymns for To-Day* (supplement to *Hymns Ancient and Modern*) (Clowes, 1968).

Who then are the charismatics? And it is here that the difficulties grow thickest. Probably, in the early 1960s the speaking with tongues was the classic test. This was *the* great evidence of the 'baptism in the Spirit', and the 'baptism' was the *sine qua non* of being 'renewed'. The party, or tradition, undoubtedly grew on this principle.[1] There came the 'masonic' recognition of others who were 'in' and the non-recognition of others who were not. The Fountain Trust provided literature, speakers, conferences on this basis. There was a mission to the church, particularly perhaps to the Church of England, and most noticeably (so it seemed) to the evangelicals. At some early stage the definition of the 'baptism' may have subtly widened —those who claimed a crisis experience of being 'flooded' with the Spirit might be deemed to be 'baptized' even if they did not speak in tongues. And in the 1970s many many persons who have simply been seeking a deeper experience of Christ, and a more consistent and satisfying spiritual life, have been found on the Fountain Trust franchise irrespective of *how* they would describe their own experience. Once a Movement like this gets going (and its initial stages are in many ways the most interesting) then after a while the original tests fade from view (though they remain part of the energizing force of the whole Movement), and those who keep company with the first generation are reckoned the charismatics of the second generation. A Movement is a movement, and its very fluidity makes it difficult to define at many points in its history. But those who have 'been around' in the Church of England for the decade or so should recognize some identifiable landmarks in the pages which follow, even if at intervals they tend to think my mapwork, compass-bearings and guide-book treatment could be done more accurately if a better man put his mind to it. I think this too!

---

[1] All the earlier writings insist (however charitably and humbly) on both the terminology and the experience. See, e.g., M. Harper *Power for the Body of Christ* (Fountain Trust, 1964) and *As at the Beginning* (Hodder, 1965) *passim;* an instance of handling exegesis to this end occurs in J. P. Baker *Baptized in One Spirit* (Fountain Trust, 1967). But the instances could be multiplied, and are matched by the early enthusiasm of more recent recruits (that term sounds awful, but can I hope be interpreted aright)—thus Colin Urquhart, in *When The Spirit Comes* (Hodder, 1974), and John Lewis, in *It Happened at the Hague* (Hodder, 1977), use the term 'baptism in the Spirit' naturally and without hesitation throughout.

## 2. WORSHIP AS THE KEY TO THE CHARISMATIC MOVEMENT

To read much of the charismatic literature which is available is very easily to get the impression that the work of the Spirit in individuals is the key to the Movement. Put together enough 'renewed' (or 'baptized in the Spirit') Christians, and you have a charismatic community or congregation. But so much of the interest has seemed to centre on the changes in the individuals, or, sometimes, in the whole lifestyle of the congregation.

On the English scene this has somehow had an inevitability to it. The doctrines of 'the baptism' and of 'gifts' have had to be related first of all to individuals. Often a group in a congregation has become charismatic without the whole congregation being affected. and thus the normal worship of the congregation has been unaffected. A specialist prayer group may have been meeting semi-underground; or direct or indirect hints may have been given from the pulpit; or some in the congregation may have gone away to special conferences; but normal worship has gone on in its own existing style.

On the other hand, where whole parishes have been affected, then the message which has come from them is often about the effect on the whole of life. There is new love, new mutual support, new outreach, new social concern—and of course wonders[1] of healing, discernment, and answered prayer. Worship has been renewed also, but this is only a part of the public account of the renewal, and it may appear less interesting to tell than the more obvious wonders which have occurred.

I believe that both these descriptions of the outcome are deceptive. The key to the Charismatic Movement is its worship, its influence upon the future is more significantly in the sphere of worship than elsewhere. and to relate other features of the Movement to its styles and content of worship is the best way to understand them all. It is true that the experience of the individual has tended to be the foundation-stone of the renewed community. It is true that the community has seen worship as simply part of the renewed life. But at heart the corporate worship is not only the outcome of the renewal of the individual, it is also the sustaining of him thereafter. And at heart, the witness and social concern of the community springs from its gathering to worship[2], especially if 'worship' can be seen, as it properly should be, not as a specially formal exercise known as 'having a service', but rather as the natural and proper agenda for the congregation or small groups when they meet. We shall see in later chapters what these agenda may be. For the moment, it is enough to

---

[1] I use the word 'wonders' as rendering the New Testament *thaumata*—the word lays emphasis upon our surprise and awe, and does not have to enter into the difficult world of definitions involved in the English word 'miracles'. Charismatics have a great sense of God's power being loose in the world in a very surprising way.

[2] It is faintly surprising to see how charismatics themselves fail to see this. Thus David Watson has written a book called *One in the Spirit* (Hodder, 1973), and, despite the title, only one chapter out of five is about 'The Holy Spirit in the Church' (pp.65-100), and this proves to be about individual gifts! Finally, on p.111(!), he writes 'In many Christian circles to-day we have neglected, to our cost, the priority of worship' (sic!). Fortunately, he *practises* the priority better than the two or three pages of his book suggest . . . The same is broadly true of Barry Kissell's *Springtime in the Church* (Hodder, 1976), and of others.

assert the centrality of the 'coming together' to an understanding of the Movement itself. There are, of course, considerably different *styles* of worship to be found within the Movement. We have already noted that in the U.S.A. it was 'high church' episcopalians who originally 'got the blessing'.[1] But in England it was largely evangelicals.[2] Both may have shared similar goals, but they came from different starting-points. Roman Catholic charismatics, who are *not* the theme of this booklet, have a different starting-place again—and 'House Church' Movements, starting *de novo* as people get together in homes and find Christ there, have a different starting-place again. And even to assert 'similar goals' may be to miss the point. The charismatics have been clear that they were to be led by the Spirit, to be shown each step as it became necessary to take it, and they have not particularly expected to have very clear goals for the future at all. Principles, yes. Blueprints, no. One congregation has of course set patterns which others can consider. An intermingling has occurred (with the Fountain Trust and other agencies 'co-ordinating') and that is how it has been one 'Movement'. But whereas the American Episcopal Church is very hot on 'programs' and Anglican evangelicals have been self-consciously working over the last fifteen years on 'policies', on the whole the charismatics have had much less of this element in them. 'Goals' is not the right terminology. Indeed, the great differentiating factor in charismatic worship has been its emphasis upon the *immediate*. It has high *experiential* expectations to meet. The presence of the Spirit it is assumed will be *felt*. And the shape, structure, content and individual roles will all have this in view.

At the gut-level this constitutes a measurable reaction. It is a reaction against the aridity of both the personal lives of individual Christians and the dryness of the public worship of many congregations. At its best, it is a dramatic warning to non-charismatics that no organization, no structuring, no texts, no music and no ministers will be any use if they do not actually bring people into touch with God. There is no substitute for encounter with the living God. At its worst, there is a cutting loose from an objective revelation of God in history, a surrender to subjective feelings of the moment, a lapse into an existentialism overlaid with Christian terminology, and thus an esoteric cult which is both incomprehensible to the outside enquirer and deaf to the outside critic. It is a matter for thanks to God that the worst is rare, and the best, or near-best, not infrequent. The dry, the organization-men, the intellectual, and the politicians—I have enough of each of these in me to recognize the description!—all are in great need of that encounter with the best of charismatic worship which is under God part of the Movement's general message to the Church of God at the present day. To worship is to meet God. And to spend time over it is not drudgery.

[1] See footnote 4 on p.6 above.

[2] There are notable exceptions, including John Gunstone, author of three books on the subject *Greater than These* (Faith Press, 1971), *The Charismatic Prayer Meeting* (Hodder, 1975), and *The Beginnings at Whatcombe* (Hodder, 1977); Colin Urquhart, author of *When the Spirit Comes* (Hodder, 1974); and (to add a more colourful touch still) Trevor Dearing, who once wrote a scholarly anglo-catholic book and is now an itinerant exorcist. There has also been a new charismatic touch associated with the Shrine at Walsingham, and I now know several clearly anglo-catholic parishes affected by the 'renewal'.

# 3. SOME IDEALS

The next stage is to draw out some major ideals on which the charismatics have been acting.

## 1. 'Body Ministry'

Charismatics have no monopoly of the concept of the 'body'[1], and they may at times apply it too narrowly to gatherings of the like-minded (which would actually be contrary to the catholicity of the Pauline teaching in 1 Corinthians 11 and 12). But, on the other hand, they have brought a dynamism into the concept which is wholly true to Paul, and has been wholly missed elsewhere. To the Parish Communion folk, the concept of 'body' has tended to suggest that the layman has a role to play (his 'liturgy' in the biblical sense) which is distinctively his—and this is worked out in worship by extending to the layman the job of not only collecting alms, but also of reading lessons, leading in intercession, 'serving' and (perhaps) assisting in the administration. Most of the lay folk still sit or stand in their places and fulfil a relatively passive and controlled 'liturgy'. After the eucharist there may be coffee for the whole congregation, but the changes are small concessions made from a very clericalist position. Charismatics on the other hand are keen to involve the whole body, with each member contributing his or her gift. Gifts—whether of tongues, prophecy, interpretation, healing, teaching, or whatever—are forms of ministry towards each other. The corporate life of the congregation is the central place for the exercise of these gifts, and times of informal and extempore prayer and praise include the opportunity for all to contribute their own gifts. Of course, the 'body-ministry' will undergird the congregational life with smaller gatherings, with care for the sick and the needy, with personal counselling (not necessarily and only on a 'clergyman-to-layman' basis), with physical work, and so on. But the characteristic note has usually been the expectation of mutual ministry in the gathering of the 'body'. In this there is both fulfilment and support and strengthening. Both those who minister and those who receive ministry feel affirmed by God as he works through this use of individual gifts in the body.

## 2. Spontaneity

The use of individual gifts requires an 'open' approach to worship. There must be opportunity for differing gifts to be exercised; time for God to speak and do new things; a freedom from the trammels of overplanning; a context for the Spirit of freedom to act. In its most absurd cartoon form this involves a theological dichotomy—the planned is man-made, mechanical, powerless, and suspect; whilst the unplanned is Spirit-given, heart-searching, powerful and welcome. To plan is to quench the Spirit; not to plan is to give him freedom.

---

[1] In particular the Liturgical Movement involved a rediscovery of the meaning of 'body' (see p.6 above), and the Ecumenical Movement has inevitably caused much wrestling with the term (for an Anglican attempt—not necessarily typical—see *Growing into Union* by four authors (S.P.C.K., 1970) pp.50ff.). But both these have been interested in the organic unity of the whole (on which charismatics have sometimes been weaker, due to their tendency towards existentialism) whereas the charismatic emphasis has been upon the context for the exercise of 'gifts'.

This *is* absurd, and is only set up that it may be seen as an Aunt Sally. Sermons are a good test case. Does the Spirit of God *not* work when men are labouring in their studies, working at the word of God, finding expression to convey that word to the hearers? And does the Spirit of God, having thus held back from the man in the study, visit that same man when he ascends the pulpit provided he has prepared nothing, but abandon him again if he proves to have prepared something? The dichotomy *is* absurd, and charismatics generally know it. Prayers (whether actually written, or drawing upon a man's memory and experiences) have roots in the past. Hymns and their music result from work in the past. Sermons, and other forms of teaching, may well take their inspiration from hard work elsewhere prior to the gathering. And the important feature of being 'open to the Spirit' in worship is to be prepared to be stirred and roused by what is already in the materials used in worship (such as hymns), as well as learning from what is in the persons taking part in worship if they prove to have a ministry to exercise. Planning ought not to be seen as the enemy of the Spirit. It conserves the benefits of the past to be the mileu of the Spirit.

In fact, charismatics have then found that a flexible rite like Series 3 communion offers a structure within which spontaneity can find an effective place. Hymns may be planned, but spontaneous singing can easily find a place; intercessions can be planned, but extemporary contributions can easily find a place; penitence can be planned, but again a mutual ministry may be exercised; the Peace may have a formal liturgical 'trigger' but all kinds of reconciliation and deepening of relationships may be prompted through its occurrence; and after communion is an obvious time for further prayer, praise and mutual encouragement. This list is nowhere near exhaustive[1], but it exemplifies the sort of use of structure-with-spontaneity which has been growing in recent years.[2]

### 3. Praise and Joy
Because charismatic worship is less cerebral and more experiential than any of the traditional ways of worship, it has to *express* the joy in the Lord which is the authentic experience of the believers. No doubt such feeling can be forced, or simulated, and there is always a danger that group pressure may cause expression to be given to what is not true contemporary experience. But all liturgical prayer and hymnsinging involves this same danger, and is different only in that other Christians will only give vent to such expression verbally, whereas charismatics want to wear it on their faces and often use their whole bodies also. But each group can easily get caught in such a group pressure.

[1] I have been present at parish worship where someone asked if she could say a word of testimony in the first five minutes of the communion service, and I have also heard 'prophecy' after the final blessing.

[2] I was at a conference recently where charismatics were specifically moved to say 'Thank you, Lord, for Series 3'! But it is also true that some freedom has been growing with the use of Series 3 in non-charismatic circles. St. John's College chapel exemplifies some meeting of the two—and so did the NEAC communion service for 2000 people in Nottingham University Sports Centre on Low Sunday 1977.

But on the assumption that we are speaking of a true joy in the Lord then it is clear that not only will this 'come through' in the singing of hymns (and the use of appropriate liturgy) it will also overflow into the 'open' periods of worship. The need for extemporary time in worship is not so much for intercession (which was a large feature of the traditional evangelical prayer meeting) as to give scope for the self-expression which a welling up joy in the Lord demands. The corporate side to this is also important—such joy communicates itself from one to another, and then back again to its source, so that a positive upwards spiral of mutual encouragement can well emerge. It is in this mood that 'singing in tongues' may well express the inexpressible, and provide a simultaneous corporate expression of the mounting complementary joy of many individuals. To speak of joy is not to disregard the elements of penitence, intercession, objective praise of God for his mighty acts, mutual ministry of various sorts, or silent and reflective meditation which all have a place. It is merely to pick on a distinguishing keynote which helps to locate charismatics as charismatics.

## 4. Community and love

This fourth keynote is neither last in order of importance, nor in actual practice separated from the other three. The concept of the body is a sharing concept. The spontaneity of experience is a shared benefit. The infectiousness of joy gathers others into the experiences of the community. In each of them the community itself is a key factor, and the life of the community stems from the shared worship.

For the charismatics, worship is meeting, and the Lord is present then in power. In that perspective, love for each other, often deeply moving in its expression, is not only thought but *felt*. This is a great undergirding factor in everything else we have to discuss.

## 4. CHARISMATIC PARTICULARS

Against the general background of the previous chapter it is worth charting some distinctive particulars.

### 1. 'Baptism in the Spirit'

The initial experience of being 'flooded' by the Spirit was regularly called the 'baptism' in the Spirit by charismatics in the 1960s.[1] A challenge was thrown down in the massive work of J. D. G. Dunn in *Baptism in the Holy Spirit* (S.C.M., 1970), where by patient and exhaustive treatment of the relevant texts on initiation and the experience of the Spirit, Dunn exploded any concept of a 'two-stage' entry into the Christian life. This was not to deny anyone's actual experience—he is too sensitive a friend of charismatics for that—but it was to deny that a second 'crisis' was truly initiatory, and it was to deny that a 'baptism' was therefore the right term for the crisis, or that the crisis could be required of anyone as a mandatory feature of the revelation of God. There has been some discussion of this crisis phenomenon in an earlier chapter[2], and it is discussed in *Gospel and Spirit*[3] in a constructive way. But for our present purposes we note that the difficulty is largely about words, and the crisis is not itself integral to corporate worship.

### 2 The gifts of the Spirit

The gifts which charismatics are keen to exercise in worship are pre-eminently tongues (with interpretation) and prophecy. These two are listed in 1 Corinthians 12.28 as examples (among others) of the way the Spirit gives different gifts to different people. Not all the gifts in that chapter are conceivably to be found in worship to-day ('apostles'?), but tongues and prophecy are the two which are discussed at length in relation to public gatherings of the church in 1 Corinthians 14. It is obvious that it is the exercise of these two 'gifts' which provides the sort of recognition-symbols which makes charismatics feel at home. In the general use of both of them the individual worshippers are in control of what they say ('the spirit of the prophets is subject to the prophets' (1 Cor. 14.31), and their speech can hardly be described as 'ecstatic'. What they have is an identifiable 'cast'—'tongues' by the use of unknown languages[4], and 'prophecy'[5] by the use of a special grammatical form ('I say unto you, my children . . .') as though God were speaking directly through the mouth of the prophets. The task here is not to evaluate these phenomena, but to chart them. When worship is 'open' these gifts take their place as normal contributions, in

[1] See p.8 above.

[2] See p.8 above.

[3] See footnote 1 on p.3 above.

[4] I am not entering into controversy here, but it is worth noting that 'tongues' has already become an institutionalized term, a special label used for nothing else. But in the New Testament there are *no* 'tongues'—only the ordinary, uninstitutionalized, term for 'languages'. But 'speaking in languages' does not have the 'special event' feel to it which 'speaking in tongues' does as a description. (This is all without prejudice to the question of how far and how often the 'gift' is genuine).

[5] For a detailed and dispassionate discussion of 'prophecy' in the Church to-day, see D. Atkinson *Prophecy* (Grove Booklet on Ministry and Worship no. 49, 1977), pp.19-23.

accordance with the provision in 1 Corinthians 14.26 'When you come together, each one has a psalm, a hymn, a tongue, an interpretation'. The theory of interpretation is that if one speaks in tongues, another will be given an interpretation which will follow the tongue. It is not so much that the interpreter will himself comprehend the tongue, as that he will feel the need to follow it with a word which is then presumed to be an interpretation.

It is not so clear which other gifts are regular features of public worship. Healing is sometimes practised in this context (for which see the next paragraph), and teaching and less distinctive forms of ministry are frequent.[1] But it seems to be tongues (with interpretation) and prophecy which are most distinctive.

## 3. The Laying on of Hands
The laying on of hands is both biblical *and* traditional. In the New Testament it is used for healing, blessing and commissioning (perhaps, but not certainly in our sense of 'ordaining'). In church history it has been used for 'confirmation' (which has often been understood to mean a special conferring of the Holy Spirit) and for ordination. But the traditional uses are highly institutionalized and are very clearly defined as being in essence ministerial—indeed episcopal—functions. The charismatics have blown this institutionalization apart in several ways:

(i) The laying on of hands is used to bring the 'baptism in the Spirit'. It is of course—as are all uses of the ceremony by all Christians— the laying on of hands *with prayer.* And the laying on of hands for the 'baptism in the Spirit' may be practised at the conclusion, or at some other suitable point, of a service designed to bring those present to see their need and to seek this experience. The ministry of laying on hands may well be exercised by any Christian in such circumstances, not only by the ordained ministers, and the same is even more true when private ministry, away from public worship, is being practised.

(ii) The laying on of hands is also used for the outward sign in the ministry of healing. This is often done in a semi-formal way at the conclusion of the distribution of communion, and those seeking healing are asked to stay at the rail—or return there—for this sort of ministry.[2] Again, the ministry may be performed by ordained persons, or by other 'elders', or by lay persons who are asked to assist in the ministry. There are other points in a service of worship where this may occur.

(iii) The laying on of hands is also used for a more general form of 'blessing' people. This can be seen as simply a variant on healing if needs of all sorts (as, e.g., psychological, spiritual and emotional) are treated as 'illnesses' needing healing. Certainly the New Testament

---

[1] Obviously 'teaching' is listed in the New Testament; so is 'giving' (Rom. 12.6-8). But as the New Testament lists are *exemplary* not *exhaustive,* it is clear that everyone's contribution to worship is a 'gift'. Charismatics are not always sure that this should be called a 'gift' but they do believe in 'body-ministry' so the contributions are welcome anyway!

[2] This is the practice in at least two parishes local to Bramcote. Compare B. Kissell *Springtime in the Church* (Hodder, 1976) p.91.

concept of 'saving' or 'making whole'[1] would support this, and the invitation to seek the ministry of healing in this way is often drawn in very broad terms so that all possible needs fall under the invitation. As discretion is necessary in such cases, and the as needs are not so overt as when cripples limp up to the front for the ministry of healing, the laying on of hands with quiet prayer, audible only to the recipient of the ministry, is far more seemly than in physical healing.

(iv) A further variant—and one which is more controversial—is the quite widespread practice of asking worshippers if they wish to receive the laying on of hands vicariously on behalf of another. The cynical might well conclude that this is a device for ensuring there are always people to seek the laying on of hands when it is offered (for all of us know *somebody* in need), but it is also clear that there are many who have valued this opportunity to give the needs of others a more clearly defined place in the worship of the congregation than simply mentioning in prayer would afford. This is particularly the case where members of the congregation (or of their families) are shut in, or in hospital, or ill a long way away, and their needs are strongly in mind for those seeking the laying on of hands. It remains arguable that this form of ministry goes beyond anything for which the New Testament gives clear warrant, but it also remains arguable that it is a perfectly legitimate extension of New Testament practice.

## 4. Bodily Contact

In one sense the laying on of hands is simply one manifestation of a much larger principle of the use of bodily contact. Part of the unfreezing of traditional worship is to become free in the use of bodies. The laying on of hands, whether formal or informal, epitomizes this. The Kiss of Peace in communion exemplifies the freedom very well, as actual kissing and hugging (between people of the same sex, as well as between the sexes) is a very warm and meaningful feature of worship (and is of course paralleled outside of worship). This is by no means exclusive to charismatics, and it raises a series of questions for all Christians. If everybody is hugged, how is special affection to be registered? And what happens when two different people approach each other with different expectations? These are problems for all sorts of Christians, but are the more involved for those whose hugs and kisses are more profound or demanding!

Not that the Kiss of Peace is the only point of contact. Whole congregations hold hands with each other at other times in worship. People hug and kiss each other at the beginning and end of worship. And the laying on of hands is simply a particular 'ministry' example of the general principle.[2] The sense of release and freedom implies an unselfconsciousness about one's body which leads naturally into meaningful (and occasionally meaningless!) contact with others. Traditional Christianity has treated touching in worship as either puerile or else a form of invasion. Charismatics have been working at the sanctification of touch.

---

[1] It will be recalled that *sozo* and *soteria* have a breadth of meanings including physical healing and eschatological salvation.

[2] Another such example, revived at St. Werburgh's Derby and perhaps elsewhere, is the Maundy Thursday 'sacrament' of foot-washing.

## 5. Ceremonial

The use of the body in worship not only involves touch of each other—it involves each worshipper's use of his own body.[1] And with charismatics it is the *whole* body. Spontaneous dancing in the aisles may be rare (outside of the West Indian Pentecostalist tradition[2], but stamping with the feet, clapping hands to the rhythm of music, doing actions along with the words of a chorus[3], and swaying the body in tune with music, or emotion, or both—these things are all common. The most distinctive ceremony of charismatics (*almost* the infallible signature or callsign!) is the lifting up of hands in praise and wonder. Sometimes this is full-arm-stretch. Sometimes it is a holding out forward of the arms with the palms open upwards, suppliant-fashion (this is more natural when kneeling or sitting). Tom Walker goes so far as to call it actual obedience.[4] It is certainly expressive.

And expression is what it is all about. Charismatic ceremonial may occasionally look like old-fashioned 'catholic' ceremonial, but the resemblance is spurious. The rationales are poles apart. Catholic ceremonial kept in existence fossilized ceremonial, of which the original *raison d'etre* was long forgotten.[5] Charismatic ceremonial is meant to express something living and dynamic. It has to have an authenticity and immediacy. Congregations do not start singing a hymn with their arms in the air—each man or woman lifts up his or her arms when 'take-off' is realized. Sometimes arms are raised in the chorus only of a hymn of which the verses are more meditative. No doubt the result can be structured into the planning of worship![6] No doubt the group pressures get strong, when all around have their arms raised. No doubt the charismatic congregations are establishing

1 And, of course, it involves such use for the non-charismatics and the anti-charismatics also. None of us can park our bodies at a meter outside of worship and go disembodied into worship. But with some worshippers one senses they either think they *have* parked their bodies or at least wish they could. Not so charismatics. To them worship includes celebrating their own incarnate state!

2 There were good scenes of this feature of West Indian Pentecostalism on a Sunday evening TV series in Spring 1977. But the charismatics under discussion here are not West Indian Pentecostalists—they are English, and Anglican, and i⁺ does make a difference!

3 I find myself in purely adult company singing and acting 'If I were a butterfly' and 'His banner over me is love'—I string along.

4 *Open to God* (Grove Booklet on Ministry and Worship no. 38, 1975) p.17.

5 Thus the chasuble apparently descended from a Roman nobleman's best dress for certain occasions, and then became a sacrificial garment (sic!), and was revived after a three hundred year gap in the Church of England to express continuity with the early church (across a gap that size?). A mitre originally related to the flames of the Holy Spirit, but now gives some pomp to a bishop without any particular reference to the Holy Spirit.

6 The cynical half of me knows what is happening when students want to sing 'I am the Bread of Life' at a communion service. They are structuring in their own spontaneous response of joy! Much was my amusement when the same request came in written form to the Congress office on the Saturday night at NEAC. It was symbolic of a desire to be released. Anyway, permission was duly granted, the song was sung (it is *Sound of Living Waters* no. 63), and the response (as planned!) was blindingly obvious. I enjoyed singing it too.

17

their own traditions which could in time fossilize. But at root, at present, the spontaneity, and the propriety of each man or woman doing his or her 'own thing'[1], are still deeply respected. Granted that, there can be a winsome loveliness in this embodied sense of praise.

## 6. Lyrics and Music

The Charismatic Movement may not have been, like Methodism, born in song. But if not, it has certainly been weaned on it. Characteristic of its songs are items from 'Come Together', from *Sounds of Living Waters* and from *Fresh Sounds.* There is almost a new culture in this distinctive style of singing.

In the first instance, the concept of 'body-ministry' has led to a widespread use of instruments. There may be all the instruments of the orchestra, some professionally played, some not, backed by children with tambourines, percussion noises, and plain handclapping—along with the universal guitars. The style simply does not admit of being confined to the organ.

Then there is the style of the music itself. It accounts for this move away from the exclusiveness of the organ, as the new compositions of the renewal are very frequently in a guitar idiom. This is the starting-point, and is demonstrated by the fact that many of the songs (as, e.g., four of the first six in *Sound of Living Waters)* have had piano parts specially arranged. This is in contrast to the *Youth Praise* idiom, where the songs were composed for the piano, and guitar chords were added later.[2] The result is that *Living Waters* songs have, on the whole, fewer chord changes than *Youth Praise* ones. In addition, the style of *Living Waters* is to use root position chords and rarely inversions, and the sumulative effect is that the music has a simplicity, a 'gentleness'[3], and a lack of the jingliness associated with the old CSSM choruses, or the slightly martial air of many of the *Youth Praise* and *Psalm Praise* compositions. Sometimes the effect of the new guitar music is very refreshing and beautiful—'beautiful' is a favourite word of romantic charismatics—sometimes it can sound trite.

The picture is completed by examining the words. Yet to examine them *on paper* may be to miss the wood for the trees. They are usually perfectly orthodox[4], with praise of Father, Son and Spirit shared evenhandedly through the collections. But reading them on paper is deceptive. Put them with their music, add in the instruments, find a congregation longing to be

---

[1] This is rather comparable to a traditional Anglican congregation where people may kneel or sit to pray without feeling under any pressure either way. There are also congregations—all too few—where worshippers may stand for the intercessions, or to receive communion, each at his or her own discretion. This sort of personal attitude need not interfere with corporateness and it is worth working at in order to make it unembarrassing to do your 'own thing'.

[2] This can lead to quite complicated chord changes.

[3] See *Sound of Living Waters* (Hodder, 1974) Foreword.

[4] But the orthodoxy is accidental, the result of a head of doctrinal steam got up long before the Charismatic Movement appeared and still with force in it. Doctrinal threefold (if not actually Trinitarian) structure is a convenient frame for, e.g., 'Father, we adore you'. Sometimes there is a lapse into sheer romanticism—e.g., 'Take our bread', written by Christians without any doctrine of eucharistic sacrifice.

released and to *express* itself in song—and the result is very different from what appears on paper. What has happened is that the cerebral content—the facts of the gospel—whilst they are still *technically* present, have yet been relegated to a low priority.[1] The syrupy 'gentleness' of the songs and choruses has become primarily a means of self-expression. It both reveals how we feel—and helps us to feel it the more. We are in love with God, and it is the feeling of it which we are stoking up.[2] So the style of singing is to repeat choruses, to sing them over and over with but one line changed each time (often with different people contributing the new line)[3], to use them to deepen the sense of being in love, and thereby at the same time to produce a great cosiness among the worshippers. In my own more critical moments I have found myself describing the new songs as 'woozy choruses'. This overstates the case—but there is a case! And I am not always in a critibal mood.

## 6. Inchoate Sacramentality

The whole use of bodies—the 'sensuousness' of Michael Harper's description[4]—is itself but a particular application of the rather 'world-affirming' stance of charismatics noted earlier.[5] Once creation is taken seriously (even if subconsciously) then a sacramental view of life is dawning. Thus it is not surprising that the eucharist has become more and more important to charismatics—whether their roots are catholic or puritan—and that the celebration of the eucharist is often happily surrounded with instruments, dance, colour and artwork. This is what I mean by an 'inchoate' sacramentality. It is not that they have worked out fresh principles from scripture and adjusted the status of the eucharist to meet it. It is rather that something almost unconscious, and certainly unselfconscious, has been happening deep down in their lives which then thrusts its way through into their style of worship. And I suspect that it is this unformed doctrine—perhaps no more than an instinct—about creation being good and being God's instrument to us of grace. This topic will bear considerable further investigation.

---

[1] Perhaps the difference is well exemplified by hearing Michael Saward's hymn 'These are the Facts' (*Psalm Praise* no. 51). Not only are the words too aggressive about 'facts' to suit the charismatic style, but the 'Brightest and Best of the Sons of the Morning' tune conveys the feel very well. Evangelical songs of the 1960s have this strong, and cerebral, element of *proclamation* of 'facts', whereas the charismatic style is to express *feelings*. To distinguish in this, admittedly overpolarized, way is not to evaluate. I suspect we need both. See also footnote no. 4 on p.21 below.

[2] In its extreme form this loses everything but feeling! One can sing 'Peace is flowing like a river' (and verses galore with 'Love' 'Joy' etc. replacing 'Peace') and never name the name of Christ, or say anything theological at all. Drug addicts, flower people, euphoric souls of any sort—all could sing this. It *has* meaning in a Christian context, but what is to set the context if the hymnbook presupposes it? This, however, is an extreme case.

[3] *Sound of Living Waters* has many such.

[4] He uses this term in a very interesting article on worship in *One in Christ* (1977, 1-2).

[5] See also p.22 below.

# 5. SOME MINOR INCIDENTALS

I want at this point to add some other perspectives which I treat in a smaller way because they are not so fundamental to the practice of worship.

## 1. Creativity

Again, this is no more than a question—but has there been a wider release of creativity than we have seen in any other Christian movement for a long time?[1] It is not only in the arts and crafts field, nor only in the music and lyrics field, nor only in the dancing and choreography field, nor only in the scripting and drama field—where does it stop? Or is this all romanticism of an ephemeral sort? One hopes there is a leavening of the whole church here. Is this part of the affirmation of creation?

## 2. Communes and community living

From the early days at Houston onwards[2], there has been a gravitation towards 'community living'. Again, there is a combination here of a simple (simplistic?) understanding of Acts, a recognition of real needs among the lonely, the one-parent families, and many others, a desire to live economically and release more members of the church for 'fulltime' service, and again this incurable and charming romanticism. It is difficult to separate out which of these motivations is uppermost in any one case. But the phenomenon of the 'commune' itself, and of several 'communes' serving and forming one local church—this is unmistakeable.

## 3. Ecumenical Worship

Because the Movement is strongly experiential, it can bring together worshippers of different denominations and traditions in one glorious whole. At times this aspect bids fair to swallow up all doctrinal differences —praise and the exercise of 'gifts' unite as nothing else will. But it is also true that a sense of denominational commitment can remain even in 'high' situations. It was a notable, and properly painful, feature of the Westminster Conference in July 1975 that Roman Catholic and non-Roman charismatics who were present went to separate communion services at the close of the Conference. The tension here will remain, and it is charismatics who will ensure it *is* a tension.

## 4. Exorcism

Exorcism is not necessarily, nor perhaps usually, performed in the context of worship. But charismatics have tended to associate the two, and certainly texts for exorcism have a liturgical cast to them. What is true is that the Charismatic Movement has led to a vastly increased interest in demonology, a vastly increased diagnosing of invasion or possession by demons, and a vastly increased practice of exorcism. This may (in its more respectable practitioners) be compared to the ministry of healing.[3]

---

[1] Since I wrote these lines my attention has been drawn to a forthcoming 'Creativity Weekend' at St. Margaret's, Aspley—a charismatic parish near St. John's College.

[2] See G. Pulkingham *Gathered for Power* (Hodder, 1974) pp.125ff; M. Harper *A New Way of Living* (Hodder, 1973) also describes the Houston community way of life. Similar experiments have been made in England in Lewsey (see C. Urquhart *When the Spirit Comes,* though Lewsey now has a new vicar), in York, and at Kennington to mention the ones which have caught my attention most recently.

[3] The most 'way out' example of charismatic-cum-exorcist (who is still Anglican) would seem to be Trevor Dearing. But the general expectation of this ministry is around— see e.g. M. Harper *Spiritual Warfare* (Hodder, 1970) and see also section H.4 of *The Nottingham Statement* (Falcon, 1977), where Michael Harper's leadership

[Continued at foot of page 21

## 6. RECENT TRENDS

It is arguable that the last few years have seen a gentle return of the charismatics from their apogee. Some of this has been described earlier[1], where it was noted that the experience of speaking in tongues was not necessarily now regarded as a *sine qua non* to be 'in' the movement, or to be credible as a 'renewed' person. It is also true that there has been a swing in places from urging the freer exercise of gifts in worship, to seeking control and disciplining of them.[2] Impatience with structures has given place to new patterns of elders (often alongside existing Anglican P.C.C. structures). And the *rapprochement* with non-charismatics has itself diminished the distinctiveness of charismatics. This is exactly the progress history would have led us to expect. A new movement thrives initially through standing apart, and developing its own life, its own style. When it is in full spate, it can afford to return to the mainstream with a view to affecting it. And this is what has happened recently. The eighteen months of dialogue leading to *Gospel and Spirit*[3], are one instance of this; the use of uncommitted persons like me in Fountain Trust Conferences and the pages of *Renewal* are another; and the actual experience of the mingling of the two at NEAC itself is a third.[4] If this last has produced what I have recently hoped and worked for—an honest conjunction of evangelicals and charismatics—then it is not only because charismatics have appeared slightly tamer than in the past. It is also, and very significantly, because evangelicals have shown greater and greater openness to the distinctive traits and insights to be found in charismatic worship.

[1] See p.8 above.

[2] I found this when I was the speaker at a residential Fountain Trust Conference at Reading in April 1976. I admittedly missed part of the conference, but whilst I was there most references to gifts in worship were *not* about how to evoke and release their ministry, but rather about how to control and discipline them! These were only passing allusions, but seemed significant to me. The same can be paralleled elsewhere. Certainly, in my experience, it has often been needed; and certainly, as far as I can see at the moment, there is a swing to treating 'prophecy' not as less than genuine, but certainly as not self-evidently relevant nor to be uncritically accepted. This is inevitable if Tom Smail's famous words, 'Two-thirds of the exercise of spiritual gifts is phoney' (Editorial in *Renewal*, Autumn 1976), are taken at their face value—charismatics are committed to sifting and testing what is delivered as prophecy. (We have tried to find a procedure for this at St. John's College where any message delivered at the Thursday evening communion—and sometimes this has been by describing a mental picture, or expressing a hope for the community, as much as by the assertive 'I the Lord say unto you . . .'—is then up for discussion by the College worship groups on the Friday, and by the staff meeting on the Monday).

[3] See footnote 1 on p.3 above.

[4] There was perhaps an interesting musical symbol of this mingling at NEAC. By both planning and coincidence (or providence) the 'theme' song of the Congress emerged as 'Jesus is Lord! Creation's voice proclaims it' ((*Sound of Living Waters* no. 82). This is a thought-provoking combination of the traditional hymn with tolerably content-ful verses, and of the joyful, repetitive and Hallelujah-ful chorus! It truly united the Congress.

---

*Continued from footnote 3 on page 20*]

of the section has led to the inclusion of a weighty paragraph on 'spiritual warfare' under the section heading of 'Christian Maturing'. The ancestry of this can be seen in his chapter of the pre-NEAC book *Obeying Christ in a Changing World: I The Lord Christ* (Collins, 1977) pp.150-1. For a not-quite-charismatic statement see J. Richards *Exorcism, Deliverance and Healing* (Grove Booklet on Ministry and Worship no. 44, 1976).

# 7. ENCOUNTERING CHARISMATIC WORSHIP

When the analysis is done, when warmer relationships have been developed, there is still a different 'feel' to charismatic worship, whether or not it reveals all the various phenomena described. Part of the purpose of this booklet is to assist understanding between two groups, so I conclude with two sets of attitudes the non-charismatic might well try to develop if and as he encounters charismatic worship.

## 1. Lessons to be learned
This heading comes first, because I genuinely believe the total impact is for the good of the Christian church, and because it is good for non-charismatics to approach an evaluation appreciatively. If the section is short it is because it repeats and summarizes points already made earlier.

(a) *A doctrine of creation.* This may not be the most obvious feature of what we encounter, nor is it necessarily well articulated by charismatics. But it is a deliverance from the negations of traditional protestant worship, and the sterility of 'sober' Anglican worship. It establishes the continuity of the churchly gathering on Sunday (or whenever) with life in the world from Monday to Saturday. It establishes the importance of buildings, settings, art, music and drama. It establishes the importance of human bodies and ceremonial and self-expression. It establishes a sacramental principle.

(b) *A doctrine of the body.* This *is* the most obvious feature of charismatics' own account of worship, and they are often better at citing the principle than acting on it! As set out in 1 Corinthians 12, it seems to demand the treating the local gathering as a body[1], and then the discovery of the gift or contribution each member is to make. The list of gifts in verse 28 is not in a ranking order, and not exclusive— it simply exemplifies variety among gifts. But the principle of the use of each person's gifts is very clear in the chapter.[2] 1 Corinthians 13 also has something to say . . .

[1] This is of course slightly different from the universal sense of 'body' given in Ephesians and Colossians, but the difference must not be exaggerated and a text like 1 Cor. 12.13 'By one Spirit we were all baptized into one body' has great supra-local implications (especially as Paul is writing from the other side of the Aegean, and using the 'we'—compare 1 Cor. 10.17).

[2] This is not perhaps the time to go into it, but I find myself intrigued by the gift in 1 Cor. 12.28 translated in the RSV as 'administrators' (Greek *kuberneseis*). J. D. G. Dunn, in *Jesus and the Spirit* (SCM, 1975) pp.252-3, suggests this gift is 'giving counsel' —for the Greek word literally means 'steering' (as in a ship). I had always thought that *my* gift was under this head as 'administration' (of which over the years I have done plenty in and out of College!). But I now wonder whether this gift is not 'steering worship'. This is exactly the gift needed in order to preside over a flexible and open liturgy—one does not 'run' nor even 'take' the service, one 'steers' it. And if this is so, then there *was* a machinery for implementing the requirements of 1 Cor. 14, and there may even have been 'ministers' of some distinctive kind. If I am right, I may still covet this gift, and it is one I would rather have than the one I thought I had in the 1960s . . .

(c) *A fusing of the vertical and horizontal.* I think this stands out clearly from the foregoing pages. There is no loss of sense of the transcendent if at the same time Christ is found in each other through a true relating to each other. There is an expectation of meeting God in all his majesty—and all his reality.

(d) *An openness to the Spirit.* The doctrine here is easy to state, less easy to act on. It is not to be equated with a loss of liturgical structure, nor should it lead to an opposition to the planning of worship. It involves having some flexibility in planning. Perhaps crucially it requires an openness of expectation. Worship is not, and will not be, the sum of the various parts we have planned. God has more for us, and we have more for him, than we anticipated whilst planning. That openness of expectation is the keynote of a dependence upon the Spirit.

Others will add their own lessons to this brief and incomplete list.

## 2. Hard questions to put

Non-charismatics who learn the four lessons above may apparently merge with the charismatic stream in Christian worship. But they should have certain insights to bring into encounter, and these they should both retain for themselves whilst learning charimsatic lessons, and should also humbly suggest to their charismatic brethren when the opportunity occurs. One of the gladdening features of the new *rapprochement* is the willingness of charismatics to learn from non-charismatics in a way which did not appear true seven years ago.

Here then are some suggested questions to be put to charismatics:

(i) *Are you retaining a firm grip on the cerebral features of Christianity?* Without the sheer hard work on the word of God (however taught and learned) the dangers of subjectivism and of existentialism are very real.

(ii) *Are you 'structuring in' certain responses, and calling them freedom?* There is strong pressure in a 'renewed' congregation both to become warmer and warmer with each other, and also to produce the right 'alleluias', the right love of choruses, the right spontaneous joy, the right deliverance from fears etc. In an insensitive congregation these responses become a form of triumphalism, and the weaker spirit must then either suffer or conform. True 'renewal' should allow people to go at their own pace.

(iii) *Are you in danger of becoming slightly cosy?* This hardly needs describing—those who have encountered this mood will recognize it as a danger. If there is overmuch holding hands and singing woozy choruses, then the very backbone of mission (and even of manhood?) may start to soften. A programme of renewed worship must march with a programme of renewed mission, and must relate to it.

(iv) *Are you in danger of taking yourselves too seriously?* This is especially a first-generation problem. Those who arrive as a tiny beachhead of renewal on the sterile wastes of Anglican worship are bound to be serious about their experience of God. They have a testimony, and it is of vital importance. The question then is whether they can both hold onto the centrality of the knowledge of God, *and* at the same time laugh at themselves. We all have to do this to live with each other in Christian fellowship—somehow we have to learn that the preacher with grotesque gestures is *both* the messenger of God *and* very funny to watch! The whole principle of the incarnation involves both God's affirmation of himself and of man—*and* his sense of humour. One of the distinguishing features of Anglican evangelicals over the last fifteen years has been their willingness to laugh at themselves.[1] Have the charismatics learned this for themselves? Can they *both* laugh at their religious culture *and* sustain it for the glory of God? If they will not laugh they become harsh in their mission. Let them not fear that by laughing (yes, even at their practice of tongues and prophecies) they will welsh on their commitment.

I should add that I am more and more sure that the answer is that the second generation[2] can and does laugh, and are thus the easier to learn from. Non-charismatics owe charismatics a certain amount of leg-pulling in order to keep them that way.

(v) *Can you be self-critical, even about your most distinctive features?* The difficulty with the sense that God is renewing a particular congregation is that it becomes hard to criticize new developments. They have an inbuilt assumption in their favour that God is at work in them. To test, or to oppose, may seem to be to withstand God. But in fact no new proposal for church life ought to be treated as revealed (even by prophecy) in such a way that it is above debate, and to debate its pros and cons is to try to discover whether it is of God, not to frustrate his will. (There is always a danger that strong characters with new proposals will pre-empt the discussion process by force of character rather than by true sensitivity to the will of God!). Being self-critical implies that what *is* happening is not necessarily what God wants to happen (it can be reformed), but that the first reform proposed is not necessarily what God wants to happen either (it can be debated on its merits).

It is a very happy time at which to write these lessons and these questions. I am no superficial optimist, but I see good signs that non-charismatics have been learning the lessons, and charismatics have been hearing the questions and acting on them. Indeed the dialogue has become both friendly and constructive. It is a real question as to whether it has not become so intimate as to rank not as a dialogue between two different parties, but a family discussion among what is actually only one party. If so, then the title must be rescinded after all and the booklet becomes 'Introducing charismatic worship'! May many participate in it.

[1] One of the distinguishing features of those who have seceded from the Church of England has been (though obviously not invariably) a lack of that sense of proportion which a keen sense of humour gives. How much laughing at themselves is done by the contributors to *The Evangelical Times?* Well, and how much by the contributors to *Renewal?* Little in the first case—ever more and more in the second, I guess. if so then dialogue can prosper.

[2] The 'second generation' may still be the same people as the 'first generation', but the 1970s provide such a different climate for them that they themselves appear as somewhat different people.